PREPARING FOR A SHOW

by
Jane Holderness-Roddam

Illustrations by
Carole Vincer

THRESHOLD BOOKS

First published in Great Britain by
Threshold Books Ltd, 661 Fulham Road,
London SW6 5PZ

Typeset by Rapid Communications Ltd, London WC1

Printed in England by Westway Offset

British Library Cataloguing in Publication Data
Holderness-Roddam, Jane
  Preparing for a show.
  1. Livestock: Horses. Showing
  I. Title
  636.1'0888

ISBN 0-901366-09-9

CONTENTS

Introduction

Clipping, grooming, trimming and plaiting, washing and travel care are all explained and illustrated, with tips on presentation and turn-out for the show ring. The equipment needed for both horse and rider is described, although this will of course vary depending on the chosen class.

Notes on training of the horse on the flat and over fences are given, as well as guidance on how to plan your day at the show.

Show preparation does require a little forward-planning and forethought but as a result your competitions will be relatively trouble-free and therefore more enjoyable. If you are lucky enough to win a rosette this will be an added bonus and something of which you can be justifiably proud. After all, it takes a lot of hard work to prepare yourself and your horse or pony for the ring, so to achieve a placing is all the more satisfying.

At some stage in their lives, most riders harbour an ambition to take part in an equestrian competition. Whether they enter a gymkhana, a show class, show jumping, dressage or any other form of equestrian competition, the thrill of actually competing in their chosen discipline can be a very rewarding experience.

Many are happy to enter a show purely for pleasure, caring little for rosettes or prizes; others use each outing as a stepping stone on the way to greater achievement, either for themselves or their horse.

The aim of this book is to offer helpful tips on how to go about preparing for a show, whatever your reasons for competing.

In the following pages we give advice on choosing appropriate classes to enter and on how to make sure that your horse will be in peak condition, healthwise, for the competitions ahead.

Choosing your class

In the horse world there are many different types of class, catering for all standards of rider and horse. Classes range from gymkhana games, where speed and athleticism win the contest, to show classes, where the horse or pony is judged for its conformation, ride and way of going. There are also show jumping classes, where a clear round over a set course leads to a jump-off to decide the eventual winner; working hunter classes, where jumping style over a rustic course of jumps and the horse's way of going are taken into account; dressage competitions, where riders perform a set of movements in a measured arena; as well as numerous ridden and in-hand classes for the best horse or pony of a certain age, type or breed.

The first thing to decide is what classes you would like to enter. Before taking the plunge, find out what is expected in the class then assess, as honestly as you can, whether you and your horse or pony would make suitable entrants.

Having chosen your class or classes you can now set about preparing yourself and your horse so that you both have the best chance of giving a good performance on the day.

You will need to make sure that you have the correct tack and clothing, and that your horse is up to the tasks required. You will also need to learn how to turn your horse out neatly and looking really smart, and be prepared to work hard to train him and yourself, perhaps taking lessons from an experienced instructor, to the standard, required by the competition.

Looking ahead

The most important factor to be considered before attempting to take part in a competition is your horse's health. If he is not in the very best of health he will not be up to the job.

Regular grooming to keep his coat in good condition is essential, but equally so are periodic worming doses, which he will need every six to eight weeks.

His teeth will need rasping once or twice and year, and he will benefit from regular influenza vaccinations, which under some competition rules are compulsory. Protection against tetanus can be combined with the 'flu jabs – your veterinary surgeon can advise you on this.

Care of the feet and regular shoeing are vital if your horse is to be able to work properly and stay sound.

Grooming kit: **1** tack box; **2** hoof oil and brush; **3** sponge; **4** stable rubber; **5-7** body, dandy and water brushes; **8** rubber curry comb; **9** metal curry comb; **10** sweat scraper; **11** hoof pick; **12** scissors; **13** mane and tail combs.

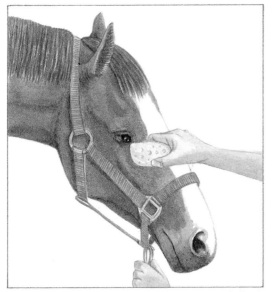

Daily spongeing of the eyes, nose and dock areas should be carried out. Keep one sponge for the face, the other for the dock. Rinse frequently.

Regular grooming will keep the coat clean, stimulate the circulation, and add to the horse's general feeling of well-being. (It is also an excellent way to get to know him.)

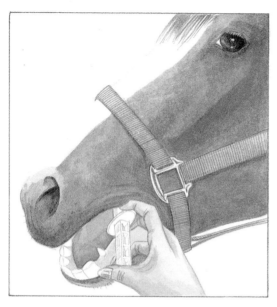

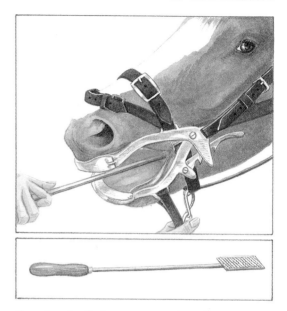

Worming is essential for your horse's general state of health. Wormers can be given in paste form (as shown) or as powders or pellets in the feed. Worm every 6-8 weeks.

Rasping teeth is necessary for effective mastication and to ensure the mouth is free from sores caused by rough edges. Check teeth every 6 months.

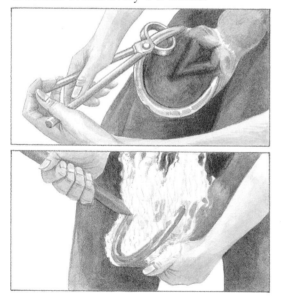

EQUINE VACCINATION CERTIFICATE

Shoeing and general care of the feet are important if your horse is to stay sound. Trimming or shoeing every 3-5 weeks and daily picking out of the feet are vital.

'Flu and tetanus vaccinations are an excellent safeguard and compulsory for many competitions. Ensure your certificates are signed and stamped correctly by the vet.

Trimming

In order to smarten up your horse's appearance you may need to tidy his whiskers and any excess hair on his jaw, nose, ears and legs.

All trimming should be done very carefully and the best results are usually achieved using either a comb and scissors (as shown) or clippers. Whichever method you use, try to make the trimming discreet, leaving the hair neat but improving the outline of the horse. Careless trimming can leave unsightly 'steps', which look worse than no trimming at all.

When trimming, start by cutting just a little at a time until the desired effect is achieved.

If using scissors make sure the blades are sharp and long. Blunt-ended scissors are much safer than pointed ones since they are unlikely to nick the horse's skin.

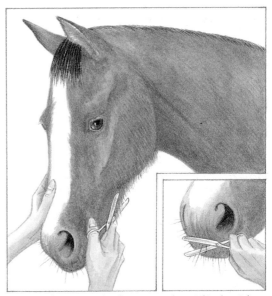

Jaw and nose whiskers can be tidied with scissors or clippers. Keep the trimming neat and discreet. Very hairy jaws require care to avoid a 'stepped' appearance.

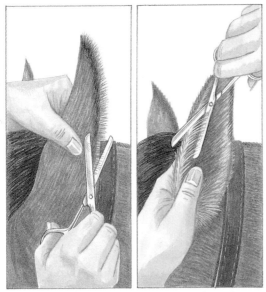

Ears may need tidying up along the edges. Use long, sharp scissors. Do not trim too much from inside the ear as you will remove nature's protection from the cold and wet.

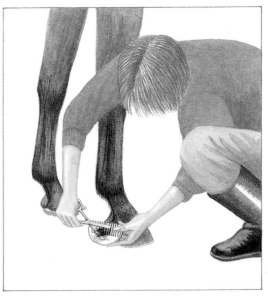

Heels and sometimes the backs of the legs require trimming. Be careful to trim the latter very discreetly – only remove 'cat' hairs and avoid cutting the actual coat.

Mane and tail pulling

Pulling your horse's mane and tail will really put the finishing touches to his appearance. Take care to do any pulling neatly and discreetly, and try to do it a little at a time so your horse does not get sore. Pulling is always easier when the horse is warm because the pores of the skin are open.

After pulling, the mane should be the same length and thickness all the way down the neck. *Never* use scissors to shorten the mane as this creates a most unnatural look.

The tail should be pulled evenly from the sides and, if necessary, from the centre until a good shape is achieved. Remember, if you wish to plait the tail you must never pull it; also it is kinder not to pull too much out of the grass-kept animal as you will take away much of his natural protection around the dock.

To pull the tail start by taking a little from either side until an even straight line is achieved. Take a little from the front but never the long hairs.

Before starting to pull the mane, comb it out carefully, have a good look at it and feel where it needs thinning and shortening. It can vary enormously.

Start pulling only a few hairs at a time and move gradually down from the top to the bottom of the neck. Always pull a dirty mane: the hair comes out more easily.

Plaiting a mane

To plait a mane well it is necessary to have it neatly and evenly pulled to a suitable length. You must take the same amount of mane for each plait, damp it thoroughly and keep an even pull throughout the plait. Turn up the end of the plait and wind the thread round it a couple of times, before folding the plait up and securing with thread. Then turn up the plait into a nice, neat ball and pass the needle though the base until the plait is firm, then cut the thread. (Use a thread that matches the colour of the horse's mane.)

Rubber bands are sometimes used, being doubled round the base of the plaited lock, then looped round the turned-up plait. Though marginally quicker to apply, rubber bands are considered unprofessional.

Plaits should not be left in too long as they can damage the mane.

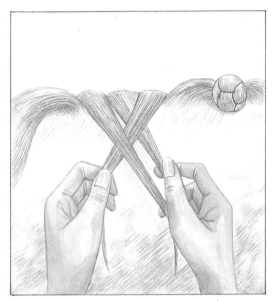

Before starting, ensure the mane is of an even length and thickness. Divide a section of the mane into three, having first damped it well, and start plaiting.

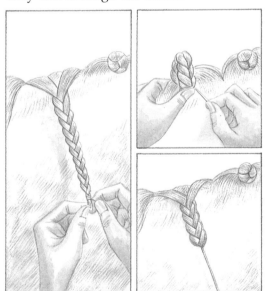

Plait evenly and firmly, secure the end well and loop up on to the neck. Secure tightly and roll up a second time to finish. Keep the mane damp and the plaiting tight.

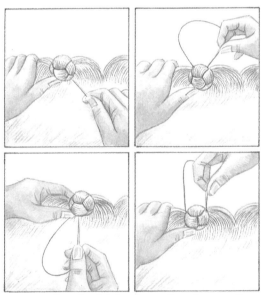

Finish off each plait by threading the needle through the completed plait a few times. Evenness in size and shape is the secret, along with tight, firm plaits.

Plaiting a tail

To plait a tail successfully, the hairs should be as long and even as possible to get a really good effect. Tail plaiting is particularly useful for grass-kept animals or those with bushy tails.

To begin, damp the hair, take a small strand from each side of the dock, pick up a third strand from one side, and work them into a central 'plait' (as shown) down the middle of the dock, taking in hair from the sides as you go. Try to keep the side pieces even and tight, and the plait straight.

When you have achieved a long enough plait (about two-thirds of the way down the dock), stop taking in hair from the sides and continue plaiting to the ends of the hairs. This long plait can then be looped back under the dock plait and stitched neatly in place.

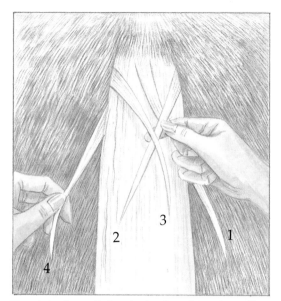

To plait the tail, begin by brushing it well then take a few strands of hair from each side of the dock. Pick up a third strand and work into a plait.

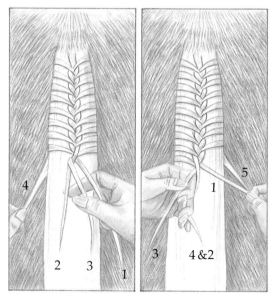

As you plait incorporate new strands from the sides, keeping the plait central, tight and even. Continue almost to the end of the dock.

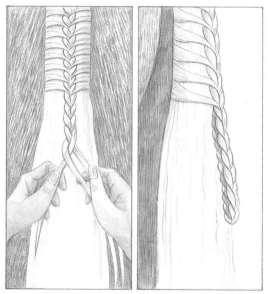

Continue forming the central plait, but without taking hair from the sides. When you reach the end, loop the plait back as shown and secure with a few stitches.

Clipping

One of the main reasons for clipping is to avoid excessive sweating and subsequent loss of condition. A clipped horse can therefore work longer, without tiring, and will dry off quicker, avoiding chills.

There are various types of clip which can be used, depending on the work and time of year. Generally, in summer it is unnecessary to clip unless a horse has a very thick coat. In winter, however, horses being worked will need some or all of their coat removed.

For the show ring, full or hunter clips look best, but for jumping or dressage any type of clip is acceptable.

The illustrations show how different areas of the horse's body are clipped. Always clip against the direction of the coat and allow the clippers to glide through the coat without effort.

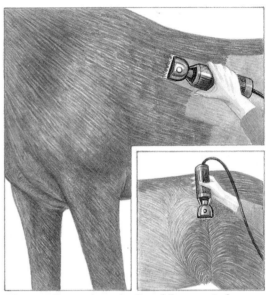

Always clip against the lie of the coat in long, slow, sweeping lines and then go lightly over it again. The hand can prevent skin twitching in awkward places.

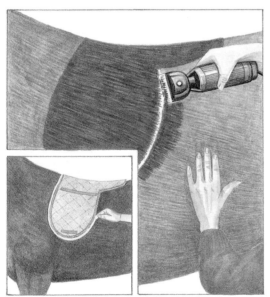

When clipping out a saddle patch, either draw the image with chalk or a little saddle soap or put a well-shaped numnah in position. Clip evenly and carefully.

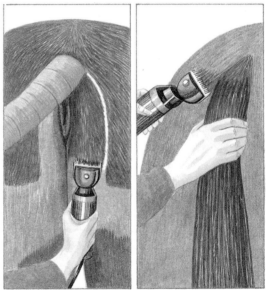

For trace and blanket clips the area round the tail is usually clipped to prevent sweating, as shown. With full clips make a triangle above the tail.

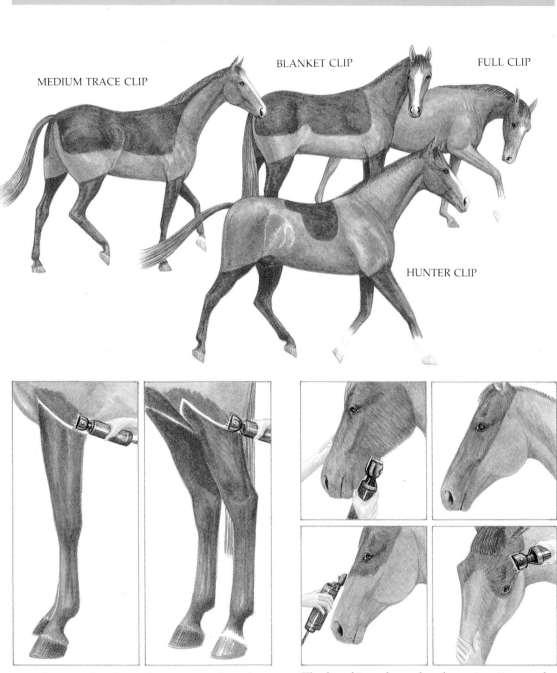

MEDIUM TRACE CLIP

BLANKET CLIP

FULL CLIP

HUNTER CLIP

With hunter clips keep the same angle at the top of the front and back legs, preferably following the line of the chest and thigh grooves, as shown.

The head is awkward and requires time and patience to get round all the angles. Difficult horses can be given a half-head clip leaving the ears and face untouched.

General training

Training of the horse is most important if the best is to be achieved.

For any class it is useful to prepare by rehearsing the routine. You should know in advance if you have to give an individual show and, if so, how you will perform it. A show should be brief and impressive and should feature walk, trot, canter (gallop, if required), and a still halt.

Strive for nice, even, smooth paces with obedience; you want the horse to be responsive and a pleasure to ride.

Many horses get a little excited by the atmosphere at shows and may need a little extra work before their class, to settle them. Also, make sure your horse is used to going near strange objects – there will be many at the ringside.

Practise for in-hand classes by running the horse up and standing him up square so he looks his best.

Train your horse to go quietly and well on the flat. Practise going past 'spooky' obstacles so that they will cause little worry in the arena. He must be a nice ride.

Lungeing can be very useful both for schooling and for quietening your horse. It can be done at the show if your horse gets a little over-excited before you ride.

For the in-hand show practise leading and running up, as well as standing the horse up correctly for the judge. Mild bits are generally used except for foals.

Training for jumping

Jumping requires practice over fences and round a course. Trotting over poles and grids will help the horse's concentration and increase his athletic ability. Cavalletti are useful as they can be used at different heights, but do not be tempted to stack them as they could roll and cause your horse to stumble.

Work at your approach to the fences and at turning into them, giving your horse enough impulsion to be able to negotiate the fence with ease. Be sure, though, to approach each fence straight. Uprights require a little care and steadying, whilst spreads generally need more impulsion. Throughout be positive but quiet with your riding.

Jump as many different types of fence as possible, including combinations, so that your horse is not put off on the day by an unusual-looking fence.

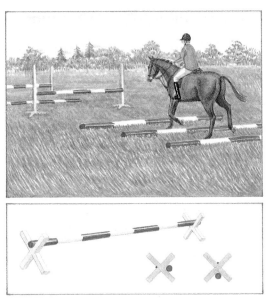

Trotting over poles and progressing to small grids of poles and jumps is a good introduction to jumping.

UPRIGHT POLES

PLANKS

GATE

WALL

PARALLEL

OXER

TRIPLE BAR

15

Preparation of the horse

As the big day draws near, the general preparation begins. Your tack should be given an extra special clean, with bits and irons polished. In summer the horse can be given a complete wash, but will probably only need his mane and tail shampooed. Be sure he does not get chilled when you do this.

The gymkhana pony does not need plaiting but the show pony or horse does, and his coat must gleam.

Make a list of all your kit for the show and tick it off as you pack it carefully into the horsebox, trailer or car.

Before you set off make sure that someone has checked the vehicle's oil, water and tyre pressures.

If you are satisfied that you are well prepared and have done your homework, you can look forward to your day at the show.

Cleaning tack and checking it is in good condition are a vital part of competing. Keep leather soft and supple and all metalwork polished. Headcollars should be polished.

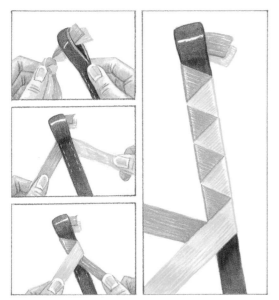

Covering a browband can be done at home using your own choice of coloured ribbon. Start at the loop, separate the ribbons and cross them over as shown.

Ready for the off! This picture shows the staggering amount of kit which is needed to go off to a show. Careful packing is necessary to fit it all in easily.

If your horse is very dirty he may need a wash. Be careful not to let him get cold and keep him warm afterwards. Do not wash him if it is cold or unnecessary.

If you wash the horse all over do the body first then rug him up before finishing off the tail and legs. Often, only the legs, mane and tail are necessary.

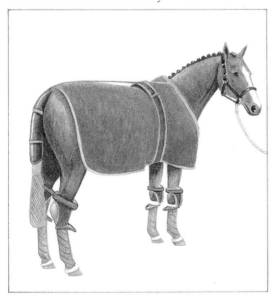

Protect your horse for travelling with knee pads, leg bandages or travelling boots and a tail guard. Keep his tail clean with a bandage. Cover him with a rug or sheet.

The gymkhana pony will not require so much travelling gear but should always have a tail bandage and boots, and a sheet if he is not a good traveller or if it is cold.

Preparation of the rider

Once the horse is clean, tidy and ready for the big day, it is the turn of the rider to prepare himself.

What you need to take with you clothes-wise depends very much on the classes you have entered but it is always better to take too much rather than too little. Your kit should always include a simple first-aid box, sewing kit and some food and drink.

The illustrations opposite may help to remind you of some of the things you should take but in addition you may need rule books, dressage test sheets, or other items appropriate to your classes.

You will certainly need a crash cap and cover for jumping classes, and should always ride with gloves and a stick. Spurs are considered correct with long boots in some adult classes but are not worn in junior show classes.

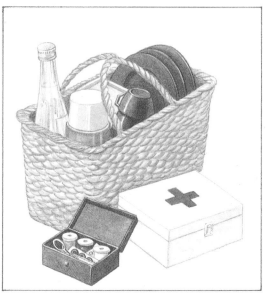

Be prepared for everying so that you get the maximum enjoyment from your day. A good picnic plus an emergency sewing and first-aid kit should see you through.

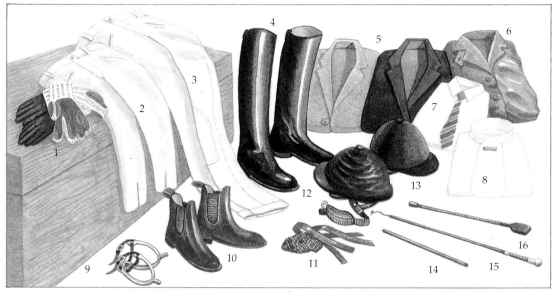

Depending on your chosen event you may need any or all of the following:
1 gloves; **2** breeches; **3** jodhpurs; **4** boots; **5** navy and tweed jackets; **6** mac; **7** shirt and tie; **8** shirt, stock and tie pin; **9** spurs; **10** jodhpur boots; **11** hairnets and ribbons; **12** crash hat and cover; **13** hunting cap; **14** show cane; **15** dressage whip; **16** jumping whip.

This rider is dressed for a **show-jumping** class at novice level. Read your rule book carefully to ensure you are correctly turned out. Crash hats are now compulsory.

In **showing** classes crash hats must be worn if there is a jumping section but ordinary hunting caps or bowlers are otherwise in order. Gloves and a show cane are correct.

For **gymkhana** games a crash hat should be worn usually with a sweater or your team colours. Saddles are not generally used. An ability to vault on to your pony is essential.

For **in-hand** classes the horse is shown in a show bridle and lead rein. A cane should be carried and the handler should be neatly dressed in jodhpurs or other smart clothing.

At the show

Once you arrive at the show there is usually a mad rush because you have failed to allow enough time for the journey. Do try to leave home in plenty of time so you can prepare yourself and your horse calmly and quietly.

You may have to find the show secretary's tent to collect your numbers or even enter for your classes so remember to take some money with you. You will also want to find out which arena you are in and when.

If jumping, go and walk the course before the class begins.

Give your horse a final brush up and oil his feet before you go into the ring. For show classes you might like to put on quarter marks or shark's teeth (as shown).

Listen out for changes in the schedule or running order or you might miss your class!

On arrival at the show it is necessary to go to the secretary's tent and collect numbers and check entries. Remember to bring the relevant paperwork.

For show-jumping classes, walk your course in plenty of time. Under BSJA rules you must be correctly dressed. Plan your approaches and check distances between fences.

The final brush-up before going into the arena is very important. For show classes the horse must be presented to the judge looking his very best.

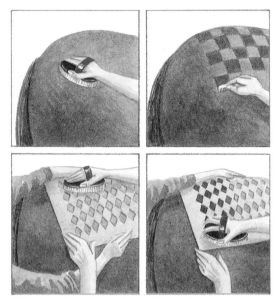

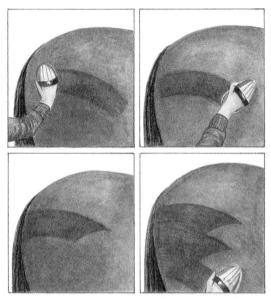

Diamonds are used in show classes except for hunters. They can be put on with a small comb, approximately 1½ ins (35mm) long, or with a special cut-out.

Shark's teeth are put on the lower part of the quarters with a damp body brush. First brush the coat naturally then use an upward stroke followed by a down one, and so on.

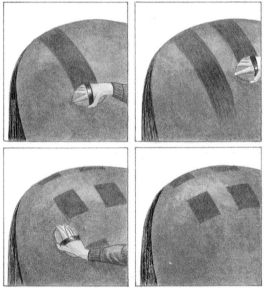

Brush two lines downwards on the quarters, then brush across at the required distance to make two or four squares.

Make sure your horse is ready on time for the class and is in the collecting ring walking round in a calm relaxed manner, so important for all showing.

Competing

When competing think carefully about what it takes to succeed in your chosen class. Speed and quick thinking are required for gymkhanas. Being in the right place to be noticed and going well are important for show classes, plus learning how to show off your horse to his best advantage. An accurate clear round will make for success in show jumping, but it will need to be coupled with speed for the jump-off. Obedience and correctness of pace are being judged in dressage, whilst in breed classes the best of each type is sought. Working hunters require correct conformation plus jumping ability.

Do not be dismayed if you do not win. Instead, watch others to see how you could improve, or perhaps seek out another type of class which would give you more of a chance.

In a **show class** make sure your horse can be easily seen by the judge. Do not let other riders come between you and the judge. Find the best place as you come past him.

Dressage tests require obedience and accurate riding. Practise beforehand and know your test. Smoothness and the correct way of going in all paces are also sought.

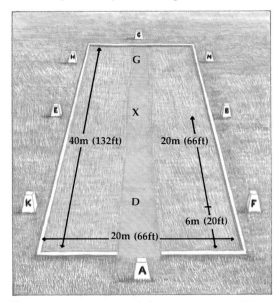

There are two sizes of dressage arena. This small one is 20 × 40m and is used for most of the less advanced tests. The large one is longer but the same width, 20 × 60m.

Gymkhana games come in many different forms, all requiring speed, balance and agility from pony and rider. Being great fun they are a wonderful start to competitive riding, and one of the ambitions of every Pony Club rider is to qualify to compete for the Prince Philip Cup at Wembley at the Horse of the Year Show every autumn.

Some shows include classes for ponies of recognised breeds or types. These may be ridden or in-hand. Many such classes offer points championships.

Working hunter classes for horses and ponies are also popular. A course of rustic fences are jumped and the best rounds go forward for further judging.

Societies and clubs

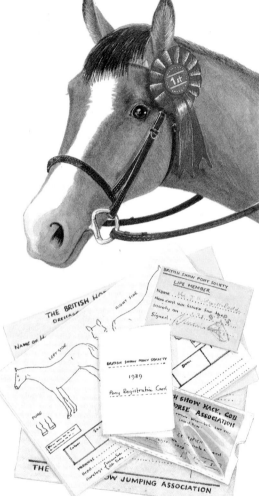

At many small shows it is quite unnecessary for you or your horse to be registered with a society or organisation, but as you progress you may like to enter classes affiliated to, say, breed societies, or show jumping or dressage groups; or you may wish to join the local Pony Club branch or a nearby riding club.

By joining a national or local equestrian society you will be kept informed of all the news and forthcoming events.

When attending bigger shows or competing for special prizes sponsored by your society, you may be required to produce certain documents, such as membership cards, height certificates, etc. So always read show schedules carefully in regard to rules and information about your particular class. Make sure you have the necessary paperwork in a handy place.

Pony Club   British Horse Society   British Show Jumping Association